Baptism in the Holy Spirit

by Duane Vander Klok

Baptism in the Holy Spirit

published by Resurrection Life Church
5100 Ivanrest Ave. S.W.
Grandville, MI 49418
616-534-4923

Unless otherwise noted,
all Scripture quotations
are from the
King James Version
of the Bible.

Cover Design: Kimberly Bonner
Text Design: Susan Harring
Revisions: Julie Johnson

ISBN 978-0-9798642-1-6

Table of Contents

Chapter 1

What is the Purpose of the Baptism in the Holy Spirit?

Baptism in the Holy Spirit

Jesus is a today God and has a present day ministry having two main functions. First, the Bible says,

"He <u>ever liveth</u> to make intercession for us" (Hebrews 7:25).

That means He's not a dead Has Been; He is a risen, living I AM who is praying for us right now! Why is He praying? Because He wants people to experience His blessings and promises in life *now*.

Jesus is the Head of the church and we are each part of the church. Whatever He as Head of the church wants to impart to us, we should want to receive. Part of His ministry today is to be the Baptizer in the Holy Spirit, so we should want that part of His ministry in our lives.

Jesus has a second ministry which began after His ascension to Heaven. John the Baptist described this part of His ministry to the people around Jerusalem who came to be baptized.

"I indeed baptize you with water unto repentance," he told them, **"but He that cometh after me is mightier than I... He [Jesus] will baptize you with the Holy Spirit and fire"** (Matthew 3:11).

Moments before He ascended to Heaven, He instructed his disciples to wait for that special gift of power:

> **"But you shall receive power when the Holy Spirit has come upon you; and you shall be witnesses unto me in Jerusalem, and in all Judaea, and in Samaria, and unto the uttermost part of the earth"** (Acts 1:8).

Note that Jesus said, **"You shall receive power..."** The baptism in the Holy Spirit is to empower us to be witnesses. Peter and the other disciples were in the upper room for ten days after the ascension praying and seeking God, but it wasn't until they were baptized in the Holy Spirit that Peter stood up, preached, and 3,000 people were saved! They had received power and it had transformed them into dynamic witnesses. Jesus said the purpose of the baptism in the Holy Spirit is to empower us to be witnesses.

Chapter 2

The Scriptural Foundation

Peter quotes the prophet Joel in Acts:

"It shall come to pass in the last days that I will pour out my Spirit upon all flesh" (Acts 2:17-18).

John the Baptist talked about it:

"I indeed baptize you with water unto repentance: but He that cometh after me is mightier than I, whose shoes I am not worthy to bear: He shall baptize you with the Holy Ghost and with fire" (Matthew 3:11).

Jesus Himself commanded His disciples in Acts 1:4-5:

"that they should not depart from Jerusalem, but wait for the promise of the Father, which, saith He, ye have heard of me. For John truly baptized with water; but ye shall be baptized with the Holy Ghost not many days hence."

Joel, John the Baptist, and Jesus talked about a baptism in the Holy Spirit, and it is mentioned throughout the New Testament. Jesus thought it so important that He commanded His disciples, "Don't leave Jerusalem without it." In modem language that means: "Don't leave the city limits without the baptism in the Holy Spirit." Why would Jesus place so much importance on the baptism in the Holy Spirit?

The reason, according to Jesus Himself, is because salvation is only the *beginning* of a new life. Jesus described salvation as a *well* when He told the Samaritan woman,

> " ... the water that I shall give him shall be in him a <u>well of water</u> springing up into everlasting life" (John 4:14).

Yet in John 7:38-39 He described something *more* when He said,

> "He that believeth on me, as the scripture hath said, out of his belly [his innermost being] shall flow <u>rivers of living water</u>. But <u>this spake He of the Spirit</u>, which they that believe on Him should receive."

Wells and rivers have different purposes. A well can take care of your *personal* need for water, but rivers can take care of the needs of *multitudes*. The baptism in the Holy Spirit gives you power—not just for your needs, but for those of multitudes.

Matthew 3:11 says Jesus wants to *baptize* believers—which literally means *immerse* them—in His Spirit. He explained the reason for this baptism in Acts 1:8:

"But ye shall receive <u>power</u>, after that the Holy Ghost is come upon you; and ye shall be <u>witnesses</u> unto me both in Jerusalem and in all Judea, and in Samaria, and unto the uttermost part of the earth."

The purpose of the baptism in the Holy Spirit is to give believers the *power to be a witness*—not to give them goose bumps and a good feeling.

I have heard people say that the baptism in the Holy Spirit was for the early church and not for today. However, the Bible never talks about the early church and the latter church. Jesus is Head of *the* church. Jesus said He would build *His* church and the gates of hell would not prevail against it. There is only one church. In fact, the Bible says in Jude 3,

"I found it necessary to write to you exhorting you to contend earnestly for the faith which was once for all delivered to the saints."

"Once for all" means God did not stop doing certain things after 100 years or 300 years. What God did in the book of Acts and in the New Testament, He is still doing today. He healed, performed miracles, delivered from demon power, and baptized in the Holy Spirit in those days, and He is doing the same today.

What God did then, He does now. What they needed then, we need now. And that is: God's Living Word, Jesus' redemptive work, and the Holy Spirit's dynamic empowerment.

Chapter 3

It Isn't Automatic

Many people say, "I received all God has for me when I got saved." That is not necessarily true. At salvation all God's promises automatically become *available* to the new believer but are not necessarily received by faith and activated in the believer's life. Acts 8 tells the story of Philip preaching in the city of Samaria and how the people listened intently to his message about the kingdom of God and watched the healing miracles happen.

"But when they believed Philip preaching the things concerning the kingdom of God, and the name of Jesus Christ, they were baptized, both men and women" (Acts 8:12).

These people had been saved because Jesus said in Mark 16:16,

"He that believeth and is baptized shall be saved."

They did and they were saved.

Yet, Acts 8:14-17 goes on to say:

"Now when the apostles which were at Jerusalem heard that Samaria had received the word of God [another way of saying they had been saved. See 1 Peter 1:23]**, they sent unto them Peter and John: who, when they had come**

down, prayed for them <u>that they might</u> <u>receive the Holy Ghost. (For as yet He</u> <u>was fallen upon none of them; only</u> <u>they were baptized in the name of the</u> <u>Lord Jesus.) Then laid they their hands</u> <u>on them, and they received the Holy</u> <u>Ghost</u>."

The apostles came from Jerusalem, laid hands on them, and *then* they were baptized in the Holy Spirit. They did not automatically receive just because they were saved. The baptism in the Holy Spirit was a second, separate experience. Just because they had been saved didn't mean they had every blessing that God wanted them to have in their lives. They definitely had not yet experienced the baptism in the Holy Spirit although they had been saved because the apostles had sent Peter and John to them for that very purpose.

Again, in Acts 19:2-6, this is,confirmed. When Paul visited Ephesus and found believers there, he asked them,

"Have ye *received* the Holy Ghost since ye believed?"

From this verse it is very clear that a person does not receive the baptism in the Holy Spirit automatically when he gets saved. Speaking of the baptism in the Holy Spirit, Paul asked if they had received Him *since* (or after) they had believed. This is a question all believers should ask themselves: "Have I received the Holy Spirit since I believed?"

At salvation the Holy Spirit comes and lives in the believer to lead and guide. However, Jesus still wants to immerse us in the Holy Spirit to give us power to be a witness.

"And they said unto him, We have not so much as heard whether there is a Holy Spirit. And when Paul had laid his hands upon them, the Holy Ghost came upon them; and they spake with tongues and prophesied."

Even though they had been saved, they still needed to receive the Holy Spirit. The fullness of His power had not automatically been given to them at salvation.

Chapter 4

The Holy Spirit Is a Gift to You

Some may say, "If God has something for me, He knows where I live and He can get it to me!" That's not the way it happens. God doesn't *force* believers to receive the Holy Spirit. In order to be received, the baptism in the Holy Spirit must be *wanted and desired.* In Acts 2:38 the people asked,

> **"What shall we do?"** Peter responded, **"Repent, and be baptized every one of you in the name of Jesus Christ for the remission of sins, and ye shall receive the <u>gift</u> of the Holy Ghost."**

The Holy Spirit is a *gift.* God is not going to give something to someone who doesn't want it.

Neither is He going to give anything that makes people act strange and weird. (I've seen people claim their weirdness is a work of the Holy Spirit, but it isn't.) Jesus says the Holy Spirit is a good gift.

> **"And I say unto you, <u>Ask, and it shall be given you</u>; seek, and ye shall find; knock, and it shall be opened unto you. For <u>everyone</u> that asketh receiveth; and he that seeketh findeth; and to him that knocketh it shall be opened. If a son shall ask bread of any of you that is a father, will he give him a stone? Or if he ask a fish, will he for a fish give**

him a serpent? Or if he shall ask an egg, will he offer him a scorpion? If ye then, being evil, know how to give good gifts unto your children; <u>how much more shall your heavenly Father give the Holy Spirit to them that ask Him?</u>" (Luke 11:9-13)

Occasionally stories will circulate about someone who heard people speaking in tongues and claimed they were praising the devil. That would make God a liar. No Christian who ever asked for the Holy Spirit received anything but the Holy Spirit. In Luke 10:19 Jesus said,

"Behold, I give unto you power to tread on serpents and scorpions, and over all the power of the enemy: and nothing shall by any means hurt you."

Bible scholars agree that the reference to serpents and scorpions in Luke 10 means Satan and demon power. If that's what it means in Luke 10, that's what it means in Luke 11 when Jesus promised to give the *Holy Spirit* to those who ask. Jesus said if you ask for a fish, you won't get a serpent. If you ask for an egg, you won't be offered a scorpion. Because both "serpent" and "scorpion" refer to demon power, Jesus is saying that we don't need to fear receiving an evil spirit when we ask our loving Heavenly Father for the baptism in the Holy Spirit.

Baptism in the Holy Spirit

Jesus said if our earthly father gives good gifts, how much more will our Heavenly Father give the Holy Spirit to those who ask Him. Therefore, if a believer asks for the Holy Spirit, he will not get some other spirit.

Chapter 5

Overcoming Misunderstandings

Baptism in the Holy Spirit

A few years ago, I received an invitation to attend an "Apostolic Succession" meeting. They said I needed to have someone lay hands on me who had had someone else lay hands on them, who had had someone else lay hands on them— all the way back to Jesus.

Wait a minute! It doesn't matter who does the laying on of hands, no one receives more of the Holy Spirit than others just because So-and-So laid hands on them. Jesus alone—not a big-name person—is the Baptizer in the Holy Spirit, whether you receive the baptism in the Holy Spirit in the privacy of a home or in a public church service. The Bible (Acts 9:11-17) tells about a certain disciple in Damascus by the name of Ananias. The Lord appeared to him in a vision and said,

> **"Arise, and go into the street which is called Straight, and enquire in the house of Judas for one called Saul, of Tarsus: for, behold, he prayeth, and hath seen in a vision a man named Ananias coming in, and putting his hand on him, that he might receive his sight."**

Now look at the next verse:

> **"And Ananias went his way and entered into the house; and putting his hands on**

him said, Brother Saul, the Lord, even Jesus, that appeared unto thee in the way as thou camest, hath sent me, that thou mightest receive thy sight, <u>and be filled with the Holy Ghost</u>."

When he laid his hands on him, Saul's sight returned, and he was filled with the Holy Spirit. Ananias was not an apostle, an evangelist, or even a pastor. Jesus is the One who baptizes in the Holy Spirit—not the person who does the laying on of hands.

This isn't the only misunderstanding that can keep people from receiving God's gift. Confusion about the supernatural can also be a hindrance. I had been saved for about a month when some of the church leaders told me about the baptism in the Holy Spirit. I wanted His Power in my life, so they gathered around and told me to lift my hands. I lifted my hands. They told me to ask God for the Holy Spirit. I did. Then they said I would speak in tongues. So I got ready. Believe it or not, I left my mouth hanging open so God could speak in tongues whenever He was ready. I waited for God to grab my tongue and go for it because I wanted it to be God, not me. About half an hour went by and those guys got tired and my mouth got very dry. They finally said, "You have received the Holy Spirit. Go home now."

I felt confused—like, what's wrong with me?

Other people receive, why don't I? I told God, "Just fill me and let me speak in tongues, and I'll read my Bible every day for the rest of my life. I'll go to church every Sunday, and pray every day, and fast once a week!" (Ever try to con God? It doesn't work!) I saw others who seemed to be so happy in their new experience with God after they had been baptized in the Holy Spirit and spoke in tongues. Why couldn't I experience that, too?

Three months later while at college, I attended a little prayer meeting and got so desperate I told God, "Okay, this is it! This is Your last chance! If You don't speak in tongues, I'm going to...This is it, God! C'mon now...I mean this is Your *very* last chance...Speak in tongues now or I'm going to!...Okay, I warned You!" I started to speak—and a new language just flowed out!

I didn't understand that when the supernatural is involved, it always has two parts: man's part and God's part. For example, when God told Moses to "Lift up your rod and stretch out your hand over the sea," that was Moses' part. He did the natural part lifting up his rod and stretching out his hand. And God did the supernatural part; He parted the waters. In the same way, when Jesus walked on the water, He told Peter, "Come." Peter did the natural part by walking, and God did the supernatural part by holding him up. When

Jesus said, "Lay hands on the sick and they will recover," we lay hands on the sick. That's the natural part. God causes them to recover; that's the supernatural part.

We do the natural, and God does the supernatural. Acts 2:4 says,

"And they were all filled with the Holy Ghost, and began to speak with other tongues, as the Spirit gave them utterance."

They began to speak, and the Spirit gave them utterance. I had been waiting for God to do all the speaking *and* giving the utterance while God had been waiting for me to begin speaking. As I sat in that college prayer meeting speaking in tongues, I realized I could've spoken in tongues back at the church months before. I could have, but I just didn't know it. I didn't understand that I had a part. I had to begin to speak in faith, and then God would give the utterance.

Someone might say, "It sounds like you turn God on and off." No, God is always on! He's always ready. You see, I can speak in Spanish or in English right now. He doesn't *make* me speak in Spanish, English, or in tongues, any more than He would *make* me pray, fast, or say no to sin. It's my choice. In I Corinthians 14:15 Paul says,

"I will pray with the spirit (tongues), **and I will pray with the understanding"** (a language he understood).

Notice he said, "I will" about *both* tongues and his own language. The individual must do the speaking.

As for our praying in the Spirit, God is ready any time, but He waits for us to start. He simply gives us the ability—but it's up to us to step out and start using it. Then He does His part.

A third misunderstanding is thinking the baptism in the Holy Spirit is a "feeling." People sometimes think their experience should be like someone else's. For example, when Aunt Susie received the baptism in the Holy Spirit, she described it as feeling like warm, liquid love pouring over her from the top of her head down to her toes. Now that doesn't mean Uncle Joe will feel the same thing when he is baptized in the Holy Spirit. Maybe he will. But maybe he won't.

So many people equate the baptism in the Holy Spirit with certain feelings, but the Holy Spirit is not a feeling. Some people get saved and feel like ten thousand pounds rolled off their shoulders. Others get saved and don't feel a thing. Did they both get saved? Yes. Neither salvation nor the baptism in the Holy Spirit is based on "feelings."

Chapter 6

Why Pray
in Tongues?

Someone might say, "I'll take the Holy Spirit, but I don't want any of those tongues." Unfortunately, that's like walking into a shoe store, picking out a pair of shoes, and telling the clerk, "I want running shoes without tongues." The clerk will shake his head at such an odd request and say, "Sorry, all our running shoes come with tongues!" The baptism in the Holy Spirit comes with tongues. It's part of the package, not something extra. Keep in mind, also, that God doesn't give useless gifts. Each has a purpose. What about speaking in tongues? What is the purpose of this gift?

1. Praying in Tongues Magnifies God

On the day of Pentecost when the Holy Spirit fell upon those in the upper room, people of fifteen different nationalities said,

"...we do hear them speak in our tongues the wonderful works of God" (Acts 2:11).

2. Praying in Tongues is Talking *to* God

Speaking in tongues is not for communicating with people but for communicating with God. According to I Corinthians 14:2, speaking in tongues is praying to God:

"For he that speaketh in an unknown tongue speaketh not unto men, but

**unto God: for no man understandeth
him; howbeit in the spirit he speaketh
mysteries."**

When you speak in tongues you are talking to
God. And all Christians agree that talking to God
is called prayer.

I Corinthians 14:14 tells us that when we pray
in tongues, our spirit prays. Normally when we
pray, our mind or understanding is praying. But
when we pray in the spirit, our spirit by the Holy
Spirit is praying directly to God.

When we speak in tongues, I Corinthians 14:2
says no one understands. You don't understand;
friends or family will not understand. However,
God understands the prayer of your spirit.

3. Praying in Tongues is Speaking in
a Divine Code

During World War II, after Americans broke
the Japanese code, they knew everything the
Japanese were going to do before they did it. This
helped America win the war. Speaking in tongues
is a prayer language Satan can *never* decode, so
he *cannot* win the battle!

That explains why praying in tongues is such
a powerful prayer weapon. I Corinthians 14:15
says:

"What is it then? I will pray with the spirit, and <u>I will pray with the understanding also</u>."

God is revealing an extremely effective and accurate weapon of prayer. *Start* praying with the spirit (in tongues, without understanding), *then* pray in English and often your thoughts on how to pray will be the interpretation of what you prayed in tongues.

Let's suppose, for example, some friends are having marital problems. The tendency is to tell God how to fix it; but God says to pray in the spirit. After praying for the situation in tongues, pray in English. Oftentimes a thought will come to mind (the understanding), which aims the prayer in exactly the right direction. Perhaps it might be something like, "Sexual abuse. Six years old." With understanding—and confidence—a prayer for healing of a damaged and broken heart caused by sexual abuse can be made on their behalf.

Now where did such thoughts come from? From the Holy Spirit giving the interpretation of what had just been prayed in the spirit. The Holy Spirit knows the mind of God, so praying in the spirit allows Him to aim our prayers in the right direction and "hit the target."

No wonder Satan has caused so much division over this gift! He doesn't like to have believers praying in the spirit for three reasons: 1) He can't decode those prayers so he can't sabotage them; 2) he can't sidetrack them; and 3) he can't shift those prayers into a selfish mode.

Sadly, in some churches speaking in tongues invites "the left foot of fellowship." Immediately! They think it's of the devil. How amazing! I served the devil for 20 years, and all the time I was drunk in the bar and running around, the devil never let me speak in tongues. But when I got saved and I'm serving God, reading my Bible, praying, fasting, worshiping Him, and I receive the baptism in the Holy Spirit, I start speaking in tongues. In the Bible when someone spoke in tongues, it was evidence they had received the baptism in the Holy Spirit. Acts 10:44-46 states,

"While Peter yet spake these words, the Holy Ghost fell on all them which heard the word. And they of the circumcision which believed were astonished, as many as came with Peter, because that on the Gentiles also was poured out the gift of the Holy Ghost. For they heard them speak with tongues, and magnify God."

Remember the apostle Paul concludes all his teaching on spiritual gifts and tongues by saying,

"Forbid not to speak with tongues"
I Corinthians 14:39.

4. God Wants His People to Speak in Tongues

A look at I Corinthians 12, 13, and 14—the three chapters where tongues are talked about more than any other place in the Bible—reveals this conclusion:

"If any man think himself to be a prophet, or spiritual, let him acknowledge that the things that I write unto you are <u>the commandments of the Lord</u>. But if any man be ignorant, let him be ignorant. Wherefore, brethren, covet to prophesy, and <u>forbid not to speak with tongues</u>" (I Corinthians 14:37-39).

We are not to forbid speaking in tongues because this is something God wants believers to do!

Speaking in tongues is the easiest manifestation of the Spirit to receive. Some people say, "I'm not going to speak in tongues. I'd rather prophesy or move in the gift of faith, or in gifts of healing and miracles." Without speaking in tongues, operating in the other gifts of the Spirit is more difficult. Yielding to the Spirit of God in tongues helps the believer yield to the Spirit of God in the other gifts.

The Bible is God speaking to you and to me.

Therefore, I Corinthians 14:5 is God saying,

"I would that ye all spake with tongues."

I want to speak with tongues if for no other reason than God says He wants me to. If it is God's will for my life, I want it. I'm not going to let tradition and doctrines of men keep me from God's will for my life.

5. Praying in Tongues is Edifying

I Corinthians 14:4 gives another reason to pray in tongues:

"He that speaketh in an unknown tongue edifieth himself."

Edify means to build up. (In fact, the English word *edifice* comes from that same root word. An edifice is something that has been built up.) Jude 20 says it again,

"But ye, beloved, <u>building up</u> yourselves on your most holy faith, praying in the Holy Ghost."

In a sense, the spirit of man is like the battery in a car. Both must be charged to operate correctly. If a car's battery has been drained, the owner will ask someone with jumper cables to charge or "edify" his battery. Praying in tongues "charges" or edifies the spirit of man. Without being built up and strong inside, a believer will have a hard time going through difficulties and trials.

Here's a good example of what it means to be "edified." An evangelist in Houston decided he would pray in tongues as he made the five-hour trip to Dallas. He reasoned that if God said it would build him up, he wanted it. As he drove along praying in tongues, he got lost and arrived home much later than planned. Sitting in the driveway, he expressed his frustration to God. He had prayed five hours and didn't feel edified at all.

He felt like the Lord replied, "You are!" Puzzled, the man decided that if God said so, then he was edified—even if he didn't feel like it. He ran in the house, freshened up, and he and his wife rushed to a prayer meeting. Arriving late, they sat in the back. When a lady seated in front of them asked for prayer, the leader asked him to pray for her.

He said he extended his hand to touch her, and when he did, it felt like 10,000 volts of electricity jumped out of his hand, hit her, and knocked her down. He looked at his hand and said, "Now that's edified!" Even though he didn't feel anything physically, yet his spirit had been charged upedified—and the power of God could touch another person's life through him.

6. Praying in Tongues Will Keep You in the Love of God

People don't always appreciate or treat others kindly, so a believer has a deep need to be strong in spirit and to be kept in the love of God. Notice what Jude 20-21 says:

"But ye, beloved, building up yourselves on your most holy faith, <u>praying in the Holy Ghost, keep yourselves in the love of God</u>, looking for the mercy of our Lord Jesus Christ unto eternal life."

Spending time praying in tongues not only strengthens a believer's heart and mind against bitter, angry thoughts, it also makes him more aware of God's love for him *and* for those who mistreat him. A believer who stays in the love of God frees Him to work in the situation to bring the needed changes.

7. Praying in Tongues Enables You to Pray About Things You Don't Know About

In his book on prayer, Kenneth Hagin tells of a woman in England who felt an urgency to pray as she went to bed. Though not sure what the need was, she prayed in tongues for several hours anyway. As the urgency lifted, she saw a vision of a very sick white man being brought into a hut by a group of black people. The man died, and they covered him with a sheet. As she watched, however, he sat up as if raised from the dead and went outside where everyone began rejoicing.

She recorded this unusual experience in her diary and never thought any more about it until two years later when a guest missionary spoke at her church. She recognized him as the white man in her vision. After the service, she described to him what she had seen in the vision, and he acknowledged that it had actually happened. They compared diaries and discovered the times and dates matched.

Romans 8:26-27 explains what happened:

"for we know not what we should pray for as we ought: but the Spirit itself maketh intercession for us with groanings which cannot be uttered. And he that searcheth the hearts knoweth what is the mind of the Spirit, because he maketh intercession for the saints according to the will of God."

When you pray in tongues, the Holy Spirit can direct you to pray for people and circumstances you know nothing about.

8. Praying in Tongues Enables a Believer to Pray the Will of God

Most people's problems are located between the ears—in the mind. The mind focuses on personal feelings and opinions: "Lord, bless *me*. Help *me*. Do this for *me*. Give me *this*. Give me *that*!" The mind is always ready to tell God how to do His job.

Praying in tongues enables a believer to pray the answer instead of the problem. When praying in the spirit (praying in tongues), the human spirit and the Holy Spirit are working together in prayer. Romans 8 says the Holy Spirit always prays according to the will of God. Always. And since He knows more about the situation than anyone else, He always prays the answer to the problem. Speaking in tongues enables a believer to pray effectively for a situation because he is praying the will of God, even if his understanding (mind) is "unfruitful"—that is, even if he doesn't fully understand.

9. Praying in Tongues Will Develop Your Spirit

The Bible says man has three parts: spirit, soul, and body. A person can develop his physical body and set amazing records of endurance and skill. The world has colleges and universities where people can develop their souls (intellect).

But what about a man's spirit? How can it be developed? Look at Isaiah 28:9-11:

"Whom shall he teach knowledge? and whom shall he make to understand doctrine? them that are weaned from the milk, and drawn from the breasts. For precept must be upon precept, precept upon precept; line upon line, line upon line; here a little, and there a little: For with stammering lips and another tongue will he speak to this people."

Paul in I Corinthians 14:20-22 lets us know that "stammering lips and another tongue" is referring to speaking in tongues in the New Testament.

Speaking in tongues opens man's spirit to what God is saying in His Word, thus strengthening and developing his spirit. My favorite way to study the Bible is to read a little at a time, then speak in tongues, then read a little more, then speak in tongues. Believers will get more revelation from God's Word reading it in this way than in any other way. I Corinthians 2:12 says God's Word cannot be understood without the Spirit of God.

"Now we have received, not the spirit

of the world, but the spirit which is of God; that we might know the things that are freely given to us of God."

As good food and exercise develop the body and keep it healthy, so also letting the Spirit of God teach and reveal the Word of God to us will keep our spirit strong and healthy.

Chapter 7

A Changed Life

In 1980, when Jeanie and I lived in Mexico, I received an invitation to speak on the "Baptism in the Holy Spirit" on Pentecost Sunday at a church in Tepeapulco. For three days before the service, the believers had been fasting and praying, and by Sunday morning quite a crowd had filled the sanctuary. I was seated on the platform with the pastor and elders of the church. After the singing started, the back door opened and a man entered with a woman following him. Now in this church, women didn't wear pants, but she did. Women had head coverings on, but she didn't. And women sat only on one side of the church, but she sat down on the men's side of the church. She wasn't following any of the local church's protocol, so I suspected she wasn't saved.

Later she told me she had gone to the bus stop as usual on her way to work as a beautician, but she couldn't stop the tormenting, confusing thoughts churning through her mind.

"God, my life is such a mess," she silently prayed. "It's so empty. I need You, God! I need You to do something in my life."

She noticed the man standing beside her had a black book with the words *Santa Biblia* (Holy Bible) on the cover. Suddenly this desperate woman made a decision. "I'm not going to work today," she determined, "I don't know where that man is going, but I'm going with him."

She didn't say anything, but when her bus came by, she let it pass. He waved down his bus, and she followed him aboard and sat next to him, still not saying a word. He got off; she got off. He walked two blocks and turned into a church. I saw her enter following him like a shadow. She hadn't been in the room for more than 30 seconds before tears were streaming down her face.

I spoke about the Holy Spirit and at the end of the service invited people to come forward if they wanted to be baptized in the Holy Spirit. I figured maybe ten or twelve people would come. Instead, 120-150 people, including this woman, jumped up and came to the altar. I knew she needed to be saved before receiving the baptism in the Holy Spirit, so I led everyone in a prayer for salvation, then a prayer asking for the baptism in the Holy Spirit. I walked up to a woman and said, "I'm going to lay hands on you, and when I do, the Holy Spirit will come on you, and you will begin to speak in tongues." No sooner had I laid my hand on her head than her hands shot up in the air, and she burst out speaking in tongues—loud! The believers still in their seats got excited and began to pray in tongues until the place sounded like Niagara Falls. One after another—including the woman who had just gotten saved—people were being baptized in the Spirit and speaking in tongues as the pastors and elders laid hands on them.

I went up on the platform to get a drink and here came one of the elders with tears running down his cheeks. "I'm praying for people, and they're receiving the baptism in the Holy Spirit!" he exclaimed.

"That's good!" I told him. "That is what's supposed to happen."

"You don't understand," he cried. "I've been trying to receive the baptism in the Holy Spirit for 30 years…30 years! I'm praying for them and they are receiving the Holy Spirit and speaking in tongues. But I never have!"

He had been taught that he had to "tarry" for the Holy Spirit, and that he needed to get "holy" first. However, salvation is a gift and so is the baptism in the Holy Spirit. God doesn't give salvation because we've earned it. Neither does He give the Holy Spirit because we're so holy. No! He gives it because He's so good!

"You're going to receive the Holy Spirit right now," I told him.

He said, "Really?"

"Yes, really!" I declared. "I'm going to lay hands on you, and when I do, you're going to receive the Holy Spirit and you're going to speak in tongues." As I reached forward, his hands shot up and he started speaking in tongues. I never did get to pray for him.

What happened? His faith finally kicked in. Isn't it interesting that it had taken this believer 30 years to have enough faith to receive the baptism in the Holy Spirit, but this woman who had been saved for less than three minutes received Him immediately? God's gift is not given because of *our* goodness, but because of *His* goodness! It is not something to be earned, but a gift to be received by faith.

That day many lives changed as the power of the Holy Spirit filled believers, both old and new—just like your life will when you, too, respond to Jesus' invitation. If, like the woman in this story, the confusion and pain of life is too much to carry any more and you're ready for a change, this is your day. You can experience salvation today by praying this simple prayer from your heart.

Dear God,

I come in Jesus' Name. I believe that Jesus is Your Son, that He died on the cross and shed His precious blood to pay for my sins. I receive your forgiveness for all my sins. I believe Jesus rose again so I make Him the Lord of my life. I am not going to live to please myself any longer. I'm going to live for Jesus every day. Thank you that I'm forgiven, I'm saved, and I'm on my way to Heaven. In Jesus' Name, Amen.

If you have prayed this prayer, I encourage you to read the little booklet, *Your New Life,* that will explain how to walk in the new life God has for you.

If you want to experience the baptism in the Holy Spirit, here is another prayer you can pray:

Heavenly Father,
You say in Your Word that the Holy Spirit is a good gift and that everyone who asks for the Holy Spirit receives. I ask to be baptized in the Holy Spirit in Jesus' Name. I thank You for filling me, for empowering my life to be a witness for You, and for giving me the gift of tongues. Now, just like Paul, I will pray with my understanding (English), and I will pray with the spirit (tongues). I believe I receive right now! In Jesus' Name, Amen.

Go ahead and tell Him how much you love Him. He is a wonderful Savior. And when you run out of words in English, begin to speak out of your spirit. He understands! Remember, you begin to speak, you use your tongue and vocal cords, but He gives you the utterance.

About the Author

Duane G. Vander Klok

Pastor Duane and Jeanie Vander Klok pastor Resurrection Life Church of Grandville, Michigan. Resurrection Life Church has a weekly attendance of over 8,000. The Vander Kloks served for seven years in Mexico with an emphasis on church planting and teaching in Bible schools.

Presently Pastor Duane travels in the United States and abroad encouraging the Body of Christ with practical teaching from the Word of God. He gives oversight to many churches in Michigan and hosts a daily television program called "Walking by Faith."

The Vander Klok family includes three sons and one daughter, their spouses, and grandchildren.

If you have a need in your life and you would like us to agree with you in prayer, please call the Walking by Faith prayer line at 1-800-988-5120.

If you would like additional copies of this book or other resources by Pastor Duane Vander Klok, please contact the Word Shop Bookstore at Resurrection Life Church by calling 616-534-4923, ext. 3724. You can also shop online at www. walkingbyfaith.tv.

GET THE
JUNK
OUT OF YOUR
TRUNK

LET GO *of the* PAST
to LIVE YOUR BEST LIFE

DUANE VANDER KLOK
FOREWORD *by* JIMMY EVANS

Your heart is like a trunk—a suitcase you carry with you throughout your life. And without a doubt, nothing can hinder your spiritual growth as much as letting a little unforgiveness into your trunk. Its poison soon seeps into your relationships with God, family, and friends—and will eventually destroy you.

In *Get the Junk Out of Your Trunk*, Pastor Duane Vander Klok shows you how to recognize unforgiveness in your life, and he reveals how Scripture can help you clean out your trunk for good. In doing so, you will make room for the peace and victory God wants you to experience daily.

Favor is the "I'm-for-you!" attitude of God toward you. It is an undeserved, amazing benefit of being His child. But because many of us misunderstand the force of God's favor, we live without it.

You may feel that God's favor is absent in your life because He is withholding it. You may think you have to talk God into releasing it. But God's mighty favor is already freely given to us all!

Through biblical examples and powerful personal experience, Pastor Duane will help you realize that God means for you to enjoy His favor every day. Duane offers practical, scriptural advice on the importance of raising your expectation of favor, believing God's promises about it and letting your faith move your mouth, so you can unleash the force of favor in your life.

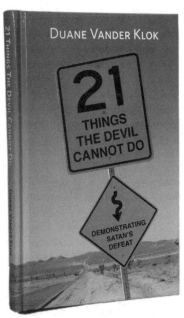

Satan is a defeated foe. Jesus came that He might "destroy the works of the devil" (1 John 3:8), and He did just that. Our job is to demonstrate Satan's defeat in our daily lives and take ground for the Kingdom of God.

"Know your enemy" is an ancient military principle that has stood the test of time, and nowhere is it more applicable than in spiritual warfare. In the midst of battle, it is important to know that the devil's weaknesses far outnumber his strengths.

Knowing all the things the devil cannot do equips us to take a firm grip on the mighty spiritual weapons Jesus gave us and wield them more effectively to secure victory over the kingdom of darkness. With Jesus the Deliverer leading us in triumph, we can show Satan how it's going to be.

DEALING WITH

Death

Biblical Answers to Questions You Weren't Ready to Ask

Duane Vander Klok

Death is an inevitable event. No other experience in life can affect us so deeply. If you have ever experienced the death of a loved one, you know the many questions that churn through one's mind. Why? Where is he? If only... Then other unavoidable questions arise demanding immediate answers. What now? Whom do we call first?

What kind of burial arrangements should we make? In His Word, God provides the answers to those questions we weren't ready to ask. I trust His Word will comfort, encourage, and strengthen you.

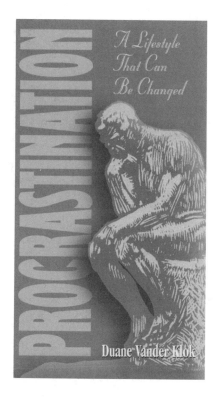

Do you procrastinate?

Do you start projects and never finish them?

Do you start a diet but never carry it past a week?

Do you have the Some Day syndrome?

If you see your God-given potential for success deteriorating into a rash of Some days—"Some day I'll deal with that problem; some day I'll get the training I need; one of these days I'll fix that broken door;"—you are a procrastinator.

The procrastination lifestyle robs you of much more than earthly success…it will affect your eternal rewards.

God has a plan for you, and Satan has a plan for you. God's plan is for abundant living. Satan's plan is for abundant misery.

Because of God's tremendous love for you, He does not leave you at the devil's mercy. He still has a plan for you and He never intended for you to fulfill Satan's plan.

Your tomorrow is determined by whose plan you choose today! What the devil decides to do to you can be reversed...choose God's plan of abundance.

Like sneering giants, problems can loom over you, haunt you, and make situations seem hopeless. As a believer in Jesus Christ, you are neither hopeless nor helpless!

God is bigger than any giant you will ever face, and He always wins. Whether your giant is failure, divorce, suicide, or bankruptcy, it is small in comparison to God. Even if all your family members for decades past have been alcoholics, abusive parents, or addicts, you can be different. You can wage war on your giants and win.

With God all things are possible. You can be a giant killer!

Asking Jesus to be your Savior is only the beginning of the Christian life. Now that you have made the most important decision of you life, your life has new meaning. But how does one go about being a Christian?

In *Your New Life*, Duane Vander Klok addresses the issues that new believers face, in a practical, straightforward way. You will find answers to your questions regarding:

- The importance of Christian friends,
- Water baptism,
- Money and the value of stewardship, and
- Being involved in a local church.

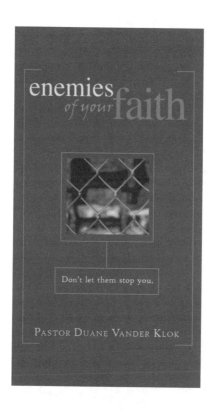

enemies *of your* faith

Don't let them stop you.

PASTOR DUANE VANDER KLOK

Don't let them stop you!

Enemies of your Faith by Pastor Duane Vander Klok is designed to help you have a strong, productive faith in God. While Satan's goal is to steal God's Word from your heart and paralyze your faith, you don't have to let him. This book will help you recognize and defeat enemies of your faith including hardness of heart, condemnation, worry, the traditions of men, and more.